50 Wyoming State Recipes for Home

By: Kelly Johnson

Table of Contents

- Bison Burger
- Wyoming Beef Jerky
- Cowboy Beans
- Rocky Mountain Oysters
- Sagebrush Stew
- Huckleberry Pie
- Elk Steak
- Buffalo Chili
- Trout Almondine
- Wyoming Whiskey BBQ Ribs
- Chokecherry Jam
- Antelope Roast
- Sage-Roasted Potatoes
- Green River Trout Tacos
- Pemmican
- Bighorn Basin Bison Chili
- Bison Meatloaf
- Western Wyoming Wild Game Stew
- Cowboy Caviar
- Wyoming Bison Sausage
- Cowboy Coffee
- Pinedale Elk Sausage Breakfast Burrito
- Wyoming Rainbow Trout Salad
- Sagebrush Smoked Salmon
- Flaming Gorge Bass Tacos
- Devil's Tower Elk Chili
- Cowboy Cobbler
- Wyoming Venison Sausage
- Bear Lake Raspberry Jam
- Buffalo Burger Sliders
- Wyoming Whiskey Glazed Salmon
- Buffalo Steak Fajitas
- Jackson Hole Bison Tenderloin
- Sagebrush Grilled Quail
- Buffalo Bolognese
- Wyoming Whiskey Smoked Brisket

- Grand Teton Elk Stew
- Green River Catfish Nuggets
- Bison Taco Salad
- Wyoming Whiskey Peach Cobbler
- Bison Breakfast Hash
- Devil's Tower Trout Cakes
- Wyoming Elk Meatballs
- Cowboy Cactus Salad
- Sagebrush Smoked Trout Dip
- Pinedale Pheasant Casserole
- Bear Lake Blueberry Pie
- Buffalo Sloppy Joes
- Wyoming Whiskey Glazed Chicken
- Bighorn Basin Bison Kabobs

Bison Burger

Ingredients:

- 1 pound ground bison meat
- 1 tablespoon Worcestershire sauce
- 1 teaspoon garlic powder
- 1 teaspoon onion powder
- 1/2 teaspoon salt
- 1/4 teaspoon black pepper
- Hamburger buns
- Optional toppings: lettuce, tomato slices, onion slices, cheese, pickles, avocado slices, bacon

Instructions:

1. In a mixing bowl, combine the ground bison meat with Worcestershire sauce, garlic powder, onion powder, salt, and black pepper. Mix gently until the seasonings are evenly distributed throughout the meat.
2. Divide the seasoned bison meat into equal portions and shape them into burger patties, about 1/2 to 3/4 inch thick. Make an indentation in the center of each patty with your thumb to prevent it from puffing up during cooking.
3. Preheat your grill or skillet over medium-high heat. If using a grill, lightly oil the grates to prevent sticking.
4. Cook the bison burgers for 4-5 minutes on each side, or until they reach your desired level of doneness. For medium-rare burgers, aim for an internal temperature of 130-135°F (54-57°C). For medium, aim for 140-145°F (60-63°C). For well-done burgers, aim for 160°F (71°C).
5. Assemble the bison burgers by placing each cooked patty on a hamburger bun. Add your desired toppings, such as lettuce, tomato slices, onion slices, cheese, pickles, avocado slices, or bacon.
6. Serve the bison burgers immediately and enjoy!

These bison burgers are juicy, flavorful, and perfect for grilling season. They pair well with a variety of toppings and condiments, so feel free to customize them to suit your taste preferences. Enjoy your delicious and nutritious bison burgers!

Wyoming Beef Jerky

Ingredients:

- 1 to 1.5 pounds beef (such as flank steak, sirloin, or top round), thinly sliced against the grain
- 1/2 cup soy sauce
- 2 tablespoons Worcestershire sauce
- 2 tablespoons honey or maple syrup
- 2 teaspoons garlic powder
- 2 teaspoons onion powder
- 1 teaspoon black pepper
- 1 teaspoon smoked paprika (optional, for a smoky flavor)
- 1/2 teaspoon liquid smoke (optional, for extra smokiness)

Instructions:

1. In a bowl or resealable plastic bag, combine the soy sauce, Worcestershire sauce, honey or maple syrup, garlic powder, onion powder, black pepper, smoked paprika (if using), and liquid smoke (if using). Mix well to combine.
2. Add the thinly sliced beef to the marinade, making sure each piece is well coated. Seal the bag or cover the bowl, and refrigerate for at least 4 hours, or preferably overnight, to allow the flavors to penetrate the meat.
3. Preheat your oven to the lowest temperature setting, typically around 175°F (80°C), or use a food dehydrator according to manufacturer instructions.
4. Remove the marinated beef from the refrigerator and drain off any excess marinade.
5. Arrange the beef slices in a single layer on wire racks placed on top of baking sheets or directly on the dehydrator trays, making sure they are not touching or overlapping.
6. If using an oven, prop the oven door open slightly to allow moisture to escape during drying.
7. Dry the beef slices in the preheated oven or food dehydrator until they are firm and chewy, about 4-6 hours, depending on thickness and desired level of doneness. Check the jerky periodically and rotate the trays if needed for even drying.
8. Once the beef jerky is done, remove it from the oven or dehydrator and let it cool completely.

9. Store the Wyoming beef jerky in an airtight container or resealable bags at room temperature for up to a few weeks. Enjoy it as a snack on the go or as a protein-rich addition to your favorite recipes!

This homemade Wyoming-style beef jerky is flavorful, tender, and perfect for fueling your adventures or satisfying your cravings for a savory snack. Adjust the seasonings and spices according to your taste preferences to create your own signature jerky recipe. Enjoy!

Cowboy Beans

Ingredients:

- 1 pound ground beef (or bacon, chopped)
- 1 onion, diced
- 2 cloves garlic, minced
- 1 can (15 ounces) kidney beans, drained and rinsed
- 1 can (15 ounces) black beans, drained and rinsed
- 1 can (15 ounces) pinto beans, drained and rinsed
- 1 can (15 ounces) diced tomatoes, undrained
- 1/4 cup ketchup
- 1/4 cup barbecue sauce
- 2 tablespoons brown sugar
- 1 tablespoon mustard
- 1 tablespoon Worcestershire sauce
- Salt and pepper to taste
- Optional toppings: shredded cheese, chopped green onions, sour cream

Instructions:

1. In a large skillet or Dutch oven, cook the ground beef (or bacon) over medium heat until browned and cooked through. If using bacon, cook until crisp, then remove from the skillet and set aside, leaving the bacon grease in the skillet.
2. Add the diced onion to the skillet and cook until softened, about 3-4 minutes. Add the minced garlic and cook for an additional 1-2 minutes.
3. Return the cooked ground beef (or crumbled bacon) to the skillet with the onions and garlic.
4. Add the drained and rinsed kidney beans, black beans, and pinto beans to the skillet, along with the undrained diced tomatoes.
5. Stir in the ketchup, barbecue sauce, brown sugar, mustard, and Worcestershire sauce until well combined.
6. Season with salt and pepper to taste, adjusting the flavors as needed.
7. Bring the mixture to a simmer, then reduce the heat to low and let it simmer for 20-30 minutes, stirring occasionally, to allow the flavors to meld and the sauce to thicken.
8. Serve the cowboy beans hot, garnished with optional toppings like shredded cheese, chopped green onions, or sour cream.

These cowboy beans are delicious served as a side dish with grilled meats, barbecue, or cornbread, or enjoyed on their own as a hearty main course. They're perfect for potlucks, picnics, or camping trips, and they can easily be customized with your favorite beans, meats, and seasonings. Enjoy!

Rocky Mountain Oysters

Ingredients:

- 1 pound Rocky Mountain oysters (bull, bison, or sheep testicles)
- 2 cups buttermilk
- 1 cup all-purpose flour
- Salt and pepper to taste
- Vegetable oil for frying
- Optional dipping sauce: cocktail sauce, ranch dressing, or aioli

Instructions:

1. Rinse the Rocky Mountain oysters under cold water and pat them dry with paper towels.
2. Using a sharp knife, carefully remove the tough outer membrane from each testicle and discard it.
3. Slice the testicles into 1/2-inch thick slices.
4. Place the sliced testicles in a bowl and cover them with buttermilk. Let them soak in the buttermilk for at least 1 hour, or preferably overnight in the refrigerator. This helps tenderize the meat and remove any gamey flavors.
5. In a shallow dish, combine the all-purpose flour with salt and pepper to taste.
6. Heat vegetable oil in a deep fryer or large, heavy-bottomed pot to 350°F (175°C).
7. Remove the Rocky Mountain oysters from the buttermilk and dredge them in the seasoned flour, shaking off any excess.
8. Carefully add the breaded testicles to the hot oil in batches, being careful not to overcrowd the fryer.
9. Fry the Rocky Mountain oysters for 3-4 minutes, or until they are golden brown and crispy.
10. Remove the fried testicles from the oil using a slotted spoon and transfer them to a plate lined with paper towels to drain any excess oil.
11. Serve the Rocky Mountain oysters hot, with your choice of dipping sauce on the side.

Rocky Mountain oysters are often served as an appetizer or snack, and they are commonly enjoyed at festivals, fairs, and events celebrating local cuisine. While they may seem unusual to some, they are considered a delicacy in many parts of the

American West and are known for their unique flavor and texture. Enjoy them if you're feeling adventurous!

Sagebrush Stew

Ingredients:

- 2 ripe bananas
- 2 eggs
- 1/4 cup honey or maple syrup
- 1/4 cup melted coconut oil or vegetable oil
- 1 teaspoon vanilla extract
- 1 cup old-fashioned rolled oats
- 1 cup whole wheat flour or all-purpose flour
- 1 teaspoon baking powder
- 1/2 teaspoon baking soda
- 1/2 teaspoon ground cinnamon
- 1/4 teaspoon salt
- Optional add-ins: chopped nuts, chocolate chips, dried fruit

Instructions:

1. Preheat your oven to 350°F (175°C). Line a muffin tin with paper liners or grease the muffin cups with cooking spray.
2. In a large mixing bowl, mash the ripe bananas with a fork until smooth.
3. Add the eggs, honey or maple syrup, melted coconut oil or vegetable oil, and vanilla extract to the mashed bananas. Stir until well combined.
4. In a separate bowl, combine the rolled oats, whole wheat flour or all-purpose flour, baking powder, baking soda, ground cinnamon, and salt. Stir to mix well.
5. Gradually add the dry ingredients to the wet ingredients, stirring until just combined. Be careful not to overmix.
6. If desired, fold in any optional add-ins such as chopped nuts, chocolate chips, or dried fruit.
7. Spoon the batter into the prepared muffin cups, filling each cup about 3/4 full.
8. Bake the muffins in the preheated oven for 18-22 minutes, or until a toothpick inserted into the center comes out clean.
9. Once baked, remove the muffins from the oven and let them cool in the muffin tin for a few minutes before transferring them to a wire rack to cool completely.
10. Serve the banana oatmeal muffins warm or at room temperature as a wholesome and delicious snack for school or work. Enjoy the moist texture and natural sweetness of these nutritious muffins!

Huckleberry Pie

Ingredients:

- 4 cups fresh huckleberries (or frozen, thawed)
- 3/4 cup granulated sugar
- 1/4 cup all-purpose flour
- 1 tablespoon lemon juice
- 1/2 teaspoon lemon zest
- 1/2 teaspoon ground cinnamon
- 1/4 teaspoon salt
- 2 tablespoons unsalted butter, cut into small cubes
- 1 egg, beaten (for egg wash)
- 1 tablespoon turbinado sugar (for sprinkling, optional)
- 1 double pie crust (store-bought or homemade)

Instructions:

1. Preheat your oven to 400°F (200°C).
2. In a large mixing bowl, combine the fresh huckleberries, granulated sugar, all-purpose flour, lemon juice, lemon zest, ground cinnamon, and salt. Stir gently until the huckleberries are evenly coated with the sugar mixture.
3. Roll out one of the pie crusts and carefully place it into a 9-inch pie dish. Trim any excess dough hanging over the edges.
4. Pour the huckleberry filling into the prepared pie crust, spreading it out evenly.
5. Dot the top of the filling with small cubes of unsalted butter.
6. Roll out the second pie crust and place it over the filling. You can either place it on top whole or create a lattice pattern by cutting strips of dough and weaving them over the filling.
7. Trim and crimp the edges of the pie crusts together to seal the pie.
8. Brush the top crust with beaten egg wash for a golden finish. If desired, sprinkle turbinado sugar over the crust for added sweetness and texture.
9. Using a sharp knife, make a few small slits in the top crust to allow steam to escape during baking.
10. Place the pie on a baking sheet to catch any drips, and then transfer it to the preheated oven.
11. Bake the huckleberry pie for 45-50 minutes, or until the crust is golden brown and the filling is bubbling.

12. Once baked, remove the pie from the oven and let it cool on a wire rack for at least 1 hour before slicing and serving.
13. Serve the huckleberry pie warm or at room temperature, optionally topped with a scoop of vanilla ice cream or whipped cream. Enjoy the sweet-tart flavor of huckleberries in this classic homemade pie!

Elk Steak

Ingredients:

- 2 elk steaks (about 8 ounces each), at room temperature
- 2 tablespoons olive oil
- 2 cloves garlic, minced
- 1 teaspoon fresh rosemary, chopped
- 1 teaspoon fresh thyme leaves, chopped
- Salt and black pepper, to taste
- Optional: additional herbs and spices of your choice

Instructions:

1. Preheat your grill to medium-high heat.
2. In a small bowl, combine the olive oil, minced garlic, chopped rosemary, and chopped thyme. Mix well to create a marinade.
3. Pat the elk steaks dry with paper towels and season them generously with salt and black pepper on both sides.
4. Place the seasoned elk steaks in a shallow dish and pour the marinade over them, making sure they are evenly coated. Allow the steaks to marinate at room temperature for about 30 minutes, or refrigerate them for up to 2 hours for a more intense flavor.
5. Once marinated, remove the elk steaks from the dish and discard any excess marinade.
6. Place the elk steaks on the preheated grill and cook them for about 4-5 minutes per side for medium-rare doneness, or adjust the cooking time according to your preference and the thickness of the steaks.
7. Avoid overcooking the elk steaks to prevent them from becoming tough and dry. Use a meat thermometer to ensure they reach an internal temperature of 130-135°F (54-57°C) for medium-rare or 140-145°F (60-63°C) for medium doneness.
8. Once cooked to your desired level of doneness, remove the elk steaks from the grill and let them rest for a few minutes before slicing.
9. Slice the elk steaks against the grain into thin slices and serve them immediately.
10. Garnish the grilled elk steaks with additional fresh herbs if desired, and serve them with your favorite side dishes such as roasted vegetables, salad, or potatoes. Enjoy the tender and flavorful elk steak straight from the grill!

Buffalo Chili

Ingredients:

- 1 lb ground buffalo meat (bison)
- 1 tablespoon olive oil
- 1 large onion, diced
- 2 cloves garlic, minced
- 1 bell pepper, diced
- 1 jalapeño pepper, seeded and diced (optional, for heat)
- 1 can (15 oz) kidney beans, drained and rinsed
- 1 can (15 oz) black beans, drained and rinsed
- 1 can (15 oz) diced tomatoes
- 1 cup beef or vegetable broth
- 2 tablespoons tomato paste
- 2 teaspoons chili powder
- 1 teaspoon ground cumin
- 1 teaspoon paprika
- 1/2 teaspoon dried oregano
- Salt and black pepper, to taste
- Optional toppings: shredded cheese, sour cream, chopped green onions, cilantro, avocado slices

Instructions:

1. Heat olive oil in a large pot or Dutch oven over medium heat. Add the diced onion and cook until softened, about 5 minutes.
2. Add the minced garlic and cook for an additional 1-2 minutes, until fragrant.
3. Add the ground buffalo meat to the pot, breaking it up with a spoon, and cook until browned and no longer pink.
4. Stir in the diced bell pepper and jalapeño pepper (if using), and cook for another 3-4 minutes.
5. Add the drained and rinsed kidney beans, black beans, diced tomatoes, beef or vegetable broth, and tomato paste to the pot. Stir to combine.
6. Season the chili with chili powder, ground cumin, paprika, dried oregano, salt, and black pepper. Adjust the seasonings to taste.
7. Bring the chili to a simmer, then reduce the heat to low. Cover and let the chili cook for about 30-40 minutes, stirring occasionally, to allow the flavors to meld together and the chili to thicken.

8. After cooking, taste the chili and adjust the seasoning if needed.
9. Serve the buffalo chili hot, ladled into bowls. Optionally, top each serving with shredded cheese, a dollop of sour cream, chopped green onions, cilantro, or avocado slices.
10. Enjoy this hearty and flavorful buffalo chili on a chilly day, with your favorite cornbread or crusty bread on the side!

Trout Almondine

Ingredients:

- 4 trout fillets (about 6-8 ounces each), skin-on
- Salt and black pepper, to taste
- 1/2 cup all-purpose flour, for dredging
- 4 tablespoons unsalted butter
- 1/2 cup sliced almonds
- 2 tablespoons fresh lemon juice
- 2 tablespoons chopped fresh parsley, for garnish
- Lemon wedges, for serving

Instructions:

1. Pat the trout fillets dry with paper towels and season them generously with salt and black pepper on both sides.
2. Dredge each trout fillet in the all-purpose flour, shaking off any excess flour.
3. In a large skillet, melt 2 tablespoons of unsalted butter over medium-high heat.
4. Once the butter is hot and foamy, add the trout fillets to the skillet, skin-side down. Cook for about 3-4 minutes, or until the skin is crispy and golden brown.
5. Carefully flip the trout fillets using a spatula and continue cooking for another 3-4 minutes on the other side, or until the fish is cooked through and flakes easily with a fork. Adjust the cooking time based on the thickness of the fillets.
6. While the trout is cooking, in a separate small skillet, melt the remaining 2 tablespoons of unsalted butter over medium heat.
7. Add the sliced almonds to the skillet and cook, stirring frequently, until the almonds are golden brown and fragrant, about 2-3 minutes. Be careful not to burn them.
8. Once the almonds are toasted, stir in the fresh lemon juice and cook for another minute, allowing the flavors to meld together.
9. Remove the skillet from the heat and spoon the almond mixture over the cooked trout fillets.
10. Garnish the trout almondine with chopped fresh parsley for a pop of color and freshness.
11. Serve the trout almondine hot, accompanied by lemon wedges for squeezing over the fish. Enjoy the delicate flavor and crunchy texture of this classic dish!

Wyoming Whiskey BBQ Ribs

Ingredients:

- 2 racks of pork baby back ribs (about 3-4 pounds each)
- Salt and black pepper, to taste
- 1 cup Wyoming Whiskey BBQ Sauce (store-bought or homemade)
- 1/4 cup Wyoming Whiskey (or bourbon of your choice)
- 2 tablespoons brown sugar
- 1 tablespoon Worcestershire sauce
- 1 teaspoon garlic powder
- 1 teaspoon onion powder
- 1/2 teaspoon smoked paprika
- Vegetable oil, for grilling

Instructions:

1. Preheat your grill to medium heat (about 300-325°F / 150-160°C).
2. Season the racks of baby back ribs generously with salt and black pepper on both sides.
3. In a small bowl, whisk together the Wyoming Whiskey BBQ sauce, Wyoming Whiskey (or bourbon), brown sugar, Worcestershire sauce, garlic powder, onion powder, and smoked paprika until well combined.
4. Place each rack of ribs on a large sheet of heavy-duty aluminum foil.
5. Pour half of the whiskey BBQ sauce mixture over each rack of ribs, spreading it evenly to coat both sides.
6. Wrap each rack tightly in the aluminum foil, creating a sealed packet.
7. Place the foil-wrapped ribs on the preheated grill and close the lid. Grill the ribs over indirect heat for about 2-2.5 hours, or until the meat is tender and easily pulls away from the bones.
8. During the last 30 minutes of cooking, carefully open the foil packets and baste the ribs with additional whiskey BBQ sauce, reserving some sauce for serving.
9. Close the foil packets and continue grilling until the ribs are nicely glazed and caramelized.
10. Once the ribs are cooked to perfection, remove them from the grill and let them rest for a few minutes before serving.
11. Slice the racks of ribs into individual portions and serve them hot, drizzled with extra Wyoming Whiskey BBQ sauce on the side.

12. Enjoy these succulent Wyoming Whiskey BBQ ribs with your favorite sides, such as coleslaw, baked beans, or cornbread, for a delicious and satisfying meal!

Chokecherry Jam

Ingredients:

- 4 cups chokecherries, pitted and stemmed
- 3 cups granulated sugar
- 1/4 cup water
- 1 tablespoon lemon juice
- 1 package (1.75 oz) powdered fruit pectin

Instructions:

1. Sterilize your canning jars and lids by boiling them in water for 10 minutes. Keep them warm until ready to use.
2. Rinse the chokecherries under cold water and remove the stems and pits.
3. In a large, heavy-bottomed pot, combine the pitted chokecherries, granulated sugar, water, and lemon juice. Stir well to combine.
4. Bring the mixture to a boil over medium-high heat, stirring frequently.
5. Once boiling, reduce the heat to medium-low and let the mixture simmer for about 15-20 minutes, stirring occasionally, until the chokecherries have softened and released their juices.
6. In a small bowl, dissolve the powdered fruit pectin in a little water according to the package instructions.
7. Stir the dissolved pectin into the simmering chokecherry mixture, stirring constantly.
8. Continue to cook the jam over medium-low heat, stirring frequently, for another 10-15 minutes, or until the mixture has thickened to your desired consistency. Keep in mind that the jam will thicken further as it cools.
9. Once the jam has reached the desired thickness, remove it from the heat.
10. Carefully ladle the hot chokecherry jam into the sterilized jars, leaving about 1/4-inch of headspace at the top.
11. Wipe the rims of the jars clean with a damp cloth to remove any spills or drips.
12. Place the lids on the jars and screw on the bands until they are fingertip tight.
13. Process the filled jars in a boiling water bath for 10 minutes to ensure proper sealing and preservation.
14. Once processed, carefully remove the jars from the water bath and let them cool completely at room temperature.

15. Check the seals on the jars by pressing down on the center of each lid. If the lid does not flex or pop, the jar is properly sealed.
16. Store the sealed jars of chokecherry jam in a cool, dark place for up to one year. Once opened, store any leftover jam in the refrigerator and use it within a few weeks.
17. Enjoy your homemade chokecherry jam on toast, biscuits, pancakes, or as a sweet topping for yogurt or ice cream!

Antelope Roast

Ingredients:

- 3-4 pounds antelope roast
- 2 tablespoons olive oil
- 2 cloves garlic, minced
- 1 onion, sliced
- 2 carrots, sliced
- 2 celery stalks, sliced
- 2 cups beef broth
- 1 cup red wine (optional)
- 2 sprigs fresh thyme
- 2 sprigs fresh rosemary
- Salt and black pepper, to taste

Instructions:

1. Preheat your oven to 325°F (160°C).
2. Season the antelope roast generously with salt and black pepper on all sides.
3. In a large Dutch oven or roasting pan, heat the olive oil over medium-high heat.
4. Sear the antelope roast on all sides until browned, about 3-4 minutes per side. Remove the roast from the pan and set it aside.
5. In the same pan, add the minced garlic, sliced onion, carrots, and celery. Cook, stirring occasionally, until the vegetables are softened and lightly browned, about 5-7 minutes.
6. Deglaze the pan with red wine (if using), scraping up any browned bits from the bottom of the pan with a wooden spoon.
7. Return the seared antelope roast to the pan, nestling it among the vegetables.
8. Pour the beef broth over the roast and vegetables, adding more liquid if necessary to partially cover the roast.
9. Add the fresh thyme and rosemary sprigs to the pan.
10. Cover the Dutch oven or roasting pan with a lid or foil and transfer it to the preheated oven.
11. Roast the antelope for about 2-3 hours, or until the meat is fork-tender and easily pulls apart.
12. Once the roast is cooked to your desired level of doneness, remove it from the oven and let it rest for about 10-15 minutes before slicing.

13. Slice the antelope roast against the grain into thin slices and serve it hot, accompanied by the roasted vegetables and pan juices.
14. Enjoy this flavorful and tender antelope roast as a hearty main dish for a special occasion or family dinner!

Sage-Roasted Potatoes

Ingredients:

- 2 pounds potatoes (such as Yukon Gold or red potatoes), washed and cut into bite-sized chunks
- 3 tablespoons olive oil
- 2 cloves garlic, minced
- 2 tablespoons fresh sage leaves, chopped
- Salt and black pepper, to taste

Instructions:

1. Preheat your oven to 400°F (200°C).
2. In a large mixing bowl, toss the potato chunks with olive oil, minced garlic, chopped sage leaves, salt, and black pepper until the potatoes are evenly coated with the seasonings.
3. Spread the seasoned potatoes in a single layer on a baking sheet lined with parchment paper or aluminum foil.
4. Place the baking sheet in the preheated oven and roast the potatoes for about 30-35 minutes, or until they are golden brown and crispy on the outside, and tender on the inside.
5. About halfway through the roasting time, carefully flip the potatoes with a spatula to ensure even cooking.
6. Once the potatoes are cooked to perfection, remove them from the oven and transfer them to a serving dish.
7. Serve the sage-roasted potatoes hot as a delicious side dish alongside your favorite main course. Enjoy the crispy exterior and flavorful sage-infused taste of these roasted potatoes!

Green River Trout Tacos

Ingredients:

- 4 trout fillets (about 6-8 ounces each), skin-on
- Salt and black pepper, to taste
- 2 tablespoons olive oil
- 8 small corn tortillas
- 1 cup shredded cabbage or coleslaw mix
- 1 avocado, sliced
- 1/4 cup chopped fresh cilantro
- Lime wedges, for serving

For the Chipotle Lime Crema:

- 1/2 cup sour cream or Greek yogurt
- 1-2 tablespoons chipotle peppers in adobo sauce, minced
- 1 tablespoon fresh lime juice
- Salt, to taste

Instructions:

1. Preheat your grill or grill pan to medium-high heat.
2. Pat the trout fillets dry with paper towels and season them generously with salt and black pepper on both sides.
3. Brush the trout fillets with olive oil to prevent sticking.
4. Place the trout fillets on the preheated grill, skin-side down. Grill for about 3-4 minutes per side, or until the fish is cooked through and flakes easily with a fork. Remove from the grill and set aside.
5. While the trout is cooking, warm the corn tortillas on the grill for about 30 seconds on each side, or until they are lightly charred and pliable. Stack the warmed tortillas and wrap them in a clean kitchen towel to keep them warm.
6. In a small bowl, prepare the chipotle lime crema by combining the sour cream or Greek yogurt, minced chipotle peppers, lime juice, and salt. Stir well to combine. Adjust the seasoning to taste.
7. To assemble the tacos, flake the grilled trout fillets with a fork and divide them evenly among the warmed tortillas.

8. Top each taco with shredded cabbage or coleslaw mix, sliced avocado, chopped cilantro, and a drizzle of chipotle lime crema.
9. Serve the Green River trout tacos immediately with lime wedges on the side for squeezing. Enjoy the fresh and flavorful combination of grilled trout and zesty toppings in these delicious tacos!

Pemmican

Ingredients:

- 2 cups lean dried meat (such as beef, venison, or bison), finely shredded or ground
- 1 cup rendered fat (such as beef tallow, suet, or lard)
- Optional: 1/4 cup dried berries (such as cranberries, blueberries, or currants)

Instructions:

1. Prepare the dried meat: If using fresh meat, thinly slice it and dry it thoroughly in a dehydrator or oven at a low temperature (around 150°F or 65°C) until completely dried and brittle. Once dried, finely shred or grind the meat into a powder using a food processor or grinder.
2. Render the fat: If using beef tallow, suet, or lard, render it by melting it in a pot over low heat until it becomes liquid. Strain out any impurities and allow the rendered fat to cool slightly.
3. In a mixing bowl, combine the dried meat with the rendered fat. The ratio of meat to fat is typically 2:1 by volume, but you can adjust it to your preference for texture and flavor.
4. If desired, stir in dried berries for added sweetness and flavor.
5. Press the pemmican mixture firmly into a shallow baking dish or mold lined with parchment paper, smoothing the surface with a spatula.
6. Allow the pemmican to cool and solidify at room temperature, or place it in the refrigerator to speed up the process.
7. Once cooled and solidified, cut the pemmican into bars or squares for easy portioning and storage.
8. Store the pemmican in an airtight container or wrap it tightly in parchment paper or plastic wrap. It will keep at room temperature for several months or longer, making it an ideal food for long-term storage or outdoor adventures.

Pemmican is a versatile food that can be eaten as is, crumbled over oatmeal or porridge, mixed into stews or soups for added protein and flavor, or enjoyed as a high-energy snack while hiking, camping, or traveling.

Bighorn Basin Bison Chili

Ingredients:

- 1 lb ground bison (buffalo)
- 1 tablespoon olive oil
- 1 onion, diced
- 3 cloves garlic, minced
- 1 bell pepper, diced (any color)
- 1 jalapeño pepper, seeded and diced (optional, for heat)
- 1 can (15 oz) kidney beans, drained and rinsed
- 1 can (15 oz) black beans, drained and rinsed
- 1 can (14.5 oz) diced tomatoes
- 1 cup beef broth
- 2 tablespoons tomato paste
- 2 tablespoons chili powder
- 1 teaspoon ground cumin
- 1 teaspoon smoked paprika
- 1/2 teaspoon dried oregano
- Salt and black pepper, to taste

Instructions:

1. In a large pot or Dutch oven, heat the olive oil over medium heat. Add the ground bison and cook until browned, breaking it up with a spoon, about 5-7 minutes.
2. Add the diced onion, minced garlic, diced bell pepper, and diced jalapeño pepper (if using) to the pot. Cook, stirring occasionally, until the vegetables are softened, about 5 minutes.
3. Stir in the drained and rinsed kidney beans, black beans, diced tomatoes, beef broth, and tomato paste.
4. Season the chili with chili powder, ground cumin, smoked paprika, dried oregano, salt, and black pepper. Stir well to combine.
5. Bring the chili to a simmer, then reduce the heat to low. Cover and let the chili simmer for about 30-40 minutes, stirring occasionally, to allow the flavors to meld together and the chili to thicken.
6. Taste the chili and adjust the seasoning if needed.
7. Once the chili is cooked to your desired consistency and flavor, remove it from the heat.

8. Serve the Bighorn Basin bison chili hot, garnished with your favorite toppings such as shredded cheese, sour cream, chopped green onions, cilantro, or avocado slices.
9. Enjoy this hearty and flavorful bison chili on a cold day, served with cornbread, rice, or tortilla chips for a delicious and satisfying meal!

Bison Meatloaf

Ingredients:

- 1 lb ground bison (buffalo)
- 1 onion, finely diced
- 2 cloves garlic, minced
- 1 bell pepper, finely diced (any color)
- 1/2 cup breadcrumbs
- 1/4 cup milk
- 1/4 cup ketchup
- 1 tablespoon Worcestershire sauce
- 1 teaspoon dried thyme
- 1 teaspoon dried oregano
- 1/2 teaspoon smoked paprika
- Salt and black pepper, to taste
- 2 eggs, beaten
- Olive oil or cooking spray, for greasing

For the Glaze:

- 1/4 cup ketchup
- 2 tablespoons brown sugar
- 1 tablespoon apple cider vinegar
- 1 teaspoon Dijon mustard

Instructions:

1. Preheat your oven to 375°F (190°C). Grease a loaf pan with olive oil or cooking spray.
2. In a large mixing bowl, combine the ground bison, finely diced onion, minced garlic, finely diced bell pepper, breadcrumbs, milk, ketchup, Worcestershire sauce, dried thyme, dried oregano, smoked paprika, salt, and black pepper. Mix until well combined.
3. Add the beaten eggs to the mixture and continue mixing until all ingredients are evenly incorporated.
4. Transfer the bison meatloaf mixture into the greased loaf pan, pressing it down evenly with a spatula.

5. In a small bowl, whisk together the ingredients for the glaze: ketchup, brown sugar, apple cider vinegar, and Dijon mustard.
6. Spread the glaze evenly over the top of the meatloaf.
7. Place the meatloaf in the preheated oven and bake for 50-60 minutes, or until the internal temperature reaches 160°F (71°C) and the top is caramelized and slightly crispy.
8. Once cooked through, remove the meatloaf from the oven and let it rest in the pan for 5-10 minutes before slicing.
9. Slice the bison meatloaf into thick slices and serve warm, accompanied by your favorite side dishes such as mashed potatoes, roasted vegetables, or a green salad.
10. Enjoy this flavorful and wholesome bison meatloaf as a comforting and satisfying meal for the whole family!

Western Wyoming Wild Game Stew

Ingredients:

- 1 lb mixed wild game meat (such as venison, elk, or bison), cubed
- 2 tablespoons olive oil
- Salt and black pepper, to taste
- 1 onion, diced
- 2 cloves garlic, minced
- 2 carrots, diced
- 2 celery stalks, diced
- 1 bell pepper, diced (any color)
- 1 can (14.5 oz) diced tomatoes
- 4 cups beef or vegetable broth
- 1 cup red wine (optional)
- 1 teaspoon dried thyme
- 1 teaspoon dried rosemary
- 1 teaspoon smoked paprika
- 1 bay leaf
- 1 cup frozen peas
- 1/4 cup chopped fresh parsley, for garnish (optional)

Instructions:

1. In a large pot or Dutch oven, heat the olive oil over medium-high heat. Add the cubed wild game meat, season with salt and black pepper, and cook until browned on all sides, about 5-7 minutes. Remove the meat from the pot and set aside.
2. In the same pot, add the diced onion, minced garlic, diced carrots, diced celery, and diced bell pepper. Cook, stirring occasionally, until the vegetables are softened, about 5 minutes.
3. Return the browned wild game meat to the pot. Add the diced tomatoes, beef or vegetable broth, red wine (if using), dried thyme, dried rosemary, smoked paprika, and bay leaf. Stir to combine.
4. Bring the stew to a simmer, then reduce the heat to low. Cover and let the stew simmer gently for about 1-1.5 hours, stirring occasionally, or until the wild game meat is tender.
5. During the last 15 minutes of cooking, add the frozen peas to the stew and stir to heat through.

6. Taste the stew and adjust the seasoning with salt and black pepper if needed.
7. Once the wild game stew is cooked to perfection, remove the bay leaf and discard.
8. Serve the Western Wyoming wild game stew hot, garnished with chopped fresh parsley if desired. Enjoy the rich and hearty flavors of this comforting stew, perfect for warming up on a chilly day in the mountains!

Cowboy Caviar

Ingredients:

- 1 can (15 oz) black beans, drained and rinsed
- 1 can (15 oz) black-eyed peas, drained and rinsed
- 1 can (15 oz) corn kernels, drained
- 1 bell pepper, diced (any color)
- 1 jalapeño pepper, seeded and finely diced
- 1/2 red onion, finely diced
- 1/4 cup chopped fresh cilantro
- 2 cloves garlic, minced
- 1 avocado, diced
- Juice of 2 limes
- 2 tablespoons olive oil
- 1 teaspoon ground cumin
- Salt and black pepper, to taste
- Tortilla chips, for serving

Instructions:

1. In a large mixing bowl, combine the black beans, black-eyed peas, corn kernels, diced bell pepper, diced jalapeño pepper, diced red onion, chopped fresh cilantro, and minced garlic.
2. Add the diced avocado to the bowl and gently toss to combine, being careful not to mash the avocado.
3. In a small bowl, whisk together the lime juice, olive oil, ground cumin, salt, and black pepper to make the dressing.
4. Pour the dressing over the cowboy caviar mixture and toss until everything is evenly coated.
5. Taste and adjust the seasoning with additional salt and black pepper if needed.
6. Cover the cowboy caviar and refrigerate for at least 30 minutes to allow the flavors to meld together.
7. Before serving, give the cowboy caviar a final stir and taste again, adjusting the seasoning if necessary.
8. Serve the cowboy caviar chilled with tortilla chips for dipping, or as a topping for tacos, grilled meats, or salads.

9. Enjoy this colorful and flavorful cowboy caviar as a refreshing appetizer or side dish, perfect for summer gatherings, picnics, or potlucks!

Wyoming Bison Sausage

Ingredients:

- 1 lb ground bison (buffalo)
- 1 teaspoon salt
- 1/2 teaspoon black pepper
- 1/2 teaspoon garlic powder
- 1/2 teaspoon onion powder
- 1/2 teaspoon smoked paprika
- 1/4 teaspoon dried thyme
- 1/4 teaspoon dried sage
- 1/4 teaspoon dried rosemary
- 1/4 teaspoon dried oregano
- Pinch of red pepper flakes (optional)
- 1 tablespoon olive oil (for cooking)

Instructions:

1. In a large mixing bowl, combine the ground bison with all the seasonings: salt, black pepper, garlic powder, onion powder, smoked paprika, dried thyme, dried sage, dried rosemary, dried oregano, and red pepper flakes (if using).
2. Use your hands or a spoon to thoroughly mix the seasonings into the ground bison until evenly distributed.
3. Once mixed, cover the bowl with plastic wrap or transfer the seasoned bison mixture to an airtight container. Refrigerate for at least 1 hour or overnight to allow the flavors to meld together.
4. After the mixture has chilled, divide it into portions and shape each portion into sausage patties or links according to your preference.
5. Heat olive oil in a skillet or frying pan over medium heat.
6. Once the skillet is hot, add the bison sausage patties or links to the pan, ensuring they are not overcrowded.
7. Cook the bison sausage for about 4-5 minutes on each side, or until they are browned and cooked through, with an internal temperature of 160°F (71°C).
8. Once cooked, remove the bison sausage from the skillet and let them rest for a few minutes before serving.

9. Serve the Wyoming bison sausage hot as a delicious and flavorful breakfast option alongside eggs, toast, or pancakes, or use it as a protein-rich ingredient in sandwiches, wraps, salads, or pasta dishes.
10. Enjoy the hearty and savory taste of Wyoming bison sausage, made with lean and flavorful bison meat!

Cowboy Coffee

Ingredients:

- 4 cups water
- 1/2 cup coarsely ground coffee beans
- Optional: pinch of salt

Instructions:

1. In a saucepan or kettle, bring the water to a rolling boil over medium-high heat.
2. Once the water is boiling, remove it from the heat and let it sit for about 30 seconds to allow it to cool slightly.
3. Add the coarsely ground coffee beans to the hot water and stir gently to combine.
4. If desired, add a pinch of salt to help enhance the flavor and reduce bitterness.
5. Cover the saucepan or kettle and let the coffee steep for about 4-5 minutes, depending on your preference for strength.
6. After steeping, carefully strain the coffee through a fine-mesh sieve or coffee filter to remove the grounds.
7. Serve the cowboy coffee hot in mugs or cups.
8. Enjoy the robust and full-bodied flavor of cowboy coffee as a classic and satisfying beverage, perfect for fueling your adventures in the great outdoors!

Pinedale Elk Sausage Breakfast Burrito

Ingredients:

- 4 large flour tortillas
- 1 lb Pinedale elk sausage (or any elk sausage), casing removed
- 6 large eggs
- 1/2 cup shredded cheddar cheese
- 1/2 cup diced bell peppers (any color)
- 1/4 cup diced onion
- Salt and black pepper, to taste
- 1 tablespoon olive oil or butter

Optional toppings:

- Salsa
- Avocado slices
- Sour cream
- Chopped fresh cilantro

Instructions:

1. Heat olive oil or butter in a large skillet over medium heat.
2. Add the diced onion and bell peppers to the skillet and cook until they are softened, about 3-4 minutes.
3. Add the elk sausage to the skillet, breaking it up with a spoon, and cook until browned and cooked through, about 5-7 minutes.
4. While the sausage is cooking, crack the eggs into a bowl and whisk them together until well beaten. Season with salt and black pepper to taste.
5. Push the sausage and vegetable mixture to one side of the skillet and pour the beaten eggs into the empty side.
6. Cook the eggs, stirring occasionally, until they are scrambled and cooked to your desired consistency, about 3-4 minutes.
7. Warm the flour tortillas in a separate skillet or in the microwave for about 10-15 seconds to make them more pliable.
8. Divide the scrambled eggs and elk sausage mixture evenly among the warmed tortillas.
9. Sprinkle shredded cheddar cheese over the top of each burrito.

10. Add any optional toppings of your choice, such as salsa, avocado slices, sour cream, or chopped fresh cilantro.
11. Roll up the tortillas tightly to form burritos, folding in the sides as you go.
12. Serve the Pinedale elk sausage breakfast burritos hot, and enjoy the hearty and flavorful combination of elk sausage, scrambled eggs, cheese, and vegetables, all wrapped up in a warm tortilla!

Wyoming Rainbow Trout Salad

Ingredients:

- 2 rainbow trout fillets (about 6-8 ounces each), skin-on
- Salt and black pepper, to taste
- 4 cups mixed salad greens (such as spinach, arugula, and mixed baby greens)
- 1 cup cherry tomatoes, halved
- 1/2 cucumber, sliced
- 1/4 red onion, thinly sliced
- 1/4 cup sliced almonds, toasted
- 1/4 cup crumbled feta cheese
- Lemon wedges, for serving

For the Lemon Herb Dressing:

- 1/4 cup extra virgin olive oil
- 2 tablespoons fresh lemon juice
- 1 teaspoon Dijon mustard
- 1 teaspoon honey or maple syrup
- 1 clove garlic, minced
- 1 tablespoon chopped fresh herbs (such as parsley, dill, or chives)
- Salt and black pepper, to taste

Instructions:

1. Preheat your grill or grill pan to medium-high heat.
2. Season the rainbow trout fillets generously with salt and black pepper on both sides.
3. Grill the trout fillets, skin-side down, for about 3-4 minutes, or until the skin is crispy and the flesh is opaque and flakes easily with a fork.
4. Carefully flip the trout fillets and grill for an additional 2-3 minutes on the other side, or until cooked through. Remove from the grill and let them cool slightly.
5. While the trout is cooling, prepare the lemon herb dressing: In a small bowl, whisk together the extra virgin olive oil, fresh lemon juice, Dijon mustard, honey or maple syrup, minced garlic, chopped fresh herbs, salt, and black pepper until well combined. Set aside.

6. In a large salad bowl, combine the mixed salad greens, halved cherry tomatoes, sliced cucumber, and thinly sliced red onion.
7. Once cooled, flake the grilled rainbow trout fillets into bite-sized pieces and add them to the salad bowl.
8. Drizzle the lemon herb dressing over the salad, tossing gently to coat everything evenly.
9. Sprinkle the toasted sliced almonds and crumbled feta cheese over the top of the salad.
10. Serve the Wyoming rainbow trout salad immediately, garnished with lemon wedges for squeezing over the fish and extra freshness.
11. Enjoy this vibrant and nutritious salad, featuring grilled rainbow trout and a zesty lemon herb dressing, perfect for a light and refreshing meal!

Sagebrush Smoked Salmon

Ingredients:

- 1 lb salmon fillet, skin-on
- 1/4 cup coarse sea salt
- 1/4 cup brown sugar
- 2 tablespoons ground black pepper
- 1 tablespoon dried sage
- 1 tablespoon dried thyme
- 1 tablespoon dried rosemary
- Olive oil, for brushing

Instructions:

1. In a small bowl, mix together the coarse sea salt, brown sugar, ground black pepper, dried sage, dried thyme, and dried rosemary to create the dry rub.
2. Pat the salmon fillet dry with paper towels and place it skin-side down on a large piece of plastic wrap or aluminum foil.
3. Rub the dry rub mixture evenly over the entire surface of the salmon fillet, ensuring it is well coated on all sides.
4. Tightly wrap the seasoned salmon fillet in the plastic wrap or aluminum foil, making sure it is sealed securely.
5. Place the wrapped salmon fillet in the refrigerator and let it cure for at least 4 hours or overnight to allow the flavors to develop.
6. After the curing process, preheat your smoker to a low temperature (around 200°F to 225°F / 95°C to 110°C) using sagebrush wood chips for smoking, if available.
7. Remove the salmon fillet from the refrigerator and unwrap it from the plastic wrap or aluminum foil.
8. Brush the exposed flesh side of the salmon fillet with olive oil to prevent sticking.
9. Place the salmon fillet directly on the smoker rack, skin-side down.
10. Close the smoker lid and smoke the salmon for about 1.5 to 2 hours, or until it is fully cooked and reaches an internal temperature of 145°F (63°C).
11. Once smoked, carefully remove the salmon from the smoker and let it rest for a few minutes before serving.
12. Serve the sagebrush smoked salmon hot or chilled, garnished with fresh herbs or lemon wedges, if desired.

13. Enjoy the rich, smoky flavor of this delicious sagebrush smoked salmon as a main dish, appetizer, or addition to salads, sandwiches, and pasta dishes!

Flaming Gorge Bass Tacos

Ingredients:

- 1 lb bass fillets (such as smallmouth or largemouth bass), skin-off
- 2 tablespoons olive oil
- 1 teaspoon smoked paprika
- 1 teaspoon ground cumin
- 1/2 teaspoon garlic powder
- 1/2 teaspoon onion powder
- Salt and black pepper, to taste
- 8 small corn or flour tortillas
- 2 cups shredded cabbage or coleslaw mix
- 1 avocado, sliced
- 1/4 cup diced red onion
- 1/4 cup chopped fresh cilantro
- Lime wedges, for serving

For the Chipotle Lime Crema:

- 1/2 cup sour cream or Greek yogurt
- 1-2 tablespoons chipotle peppers in adobo sauce, minced
- 1 tablespoon fresh lime juice
- Salt, to taste

Instructions:

1. Preheat your grill or grill pan to medium-high heat.
2. In a small bowl, mix together the olive oil, smoked paprika, ground cumin, garlic powder, onion powder, salt, and black pepper to create a marinade.
3. Pat the bass fillets dry with paper towels and brush both sides with the marinade.
4. Grill the bass fillets for about 3-4 minutes on each side, or until they are cooked through and flake easily with a fork. Remove from the grill and let them rest for a few minutes.
5. While the bass is grilling, warm the tortillas on the grill for about 30 seconds on each side, or until they are soft and pliable. Wrap them in a clean kitchen towel to keep them warm.

6. To make the chipotle lime crema, whisk together the sour cream or Greek yogurt, minced chipotle peppers, lime juice, and salt in a small bowl. Adjust the seasoning to taste.
7. Assemble the tacos by placing a portion of shredded cabbage or coleslaw mix on each tortilla.
8. Top with a grilled bass fillet, sliced avocado, diced red onion, and chopped fresh cilantro.
9. Drizzle the chipotle lime crema over the top of each taco.
10. Serve the Flaming Gorge bass tacos hot, accompanied by lime wedges for squeezing.
11. Enjoy the delicious flavors of these fresh and flavorful fish tacos, inspired by the beautiful surroundings of Flaming Gorge!

Devil's Tower Elk Chili

Ingredients:

- 1 lb ground elk meat
- 2 tablespoons olive oil
- 1 onion, diced
- 3 cloves garlic, minced
- 1 bell pepper, diced (any color)
- 2 celery stalks, diced
- 1 jalapeño pepper, seeded and diced (optional, for heat)
- 1 can (15 oz) kidney beans, drained and rinsed
- 1 can (15 oz) black beans, drained and rinsed
- 1 can (14.5 oz) diced tomatoes
- 1 cup beef broth
- 1 cup dark beer (such as stout or porter)
- 2 tablespoons tomato paste
- 2 tablespoons chili powder
- 1 teaspoon ground cumin
- 1 teaspoon smoked paprika
- 1/2 teaspoon dried oregano
- Salt and black pepper, to taste

Instructions:

1. Heat olive oil in a large pot or Dutch oven over medium-high heat.
2. Add the diced onion, minced garlic, diced bell pepper, diced celery, and diced jalapeño pepper (if using). Cook, stirring occasionally, until the vegetables are softened, about 5 minutes.
3. Add the ground elk meat to the pot. Cook, breaking it up with a spoon, until browned and cooked through, about 5-7 minutes.
4. Stir in the drained and rinsed kidney beans, black beans, diced tomatoes, beef broth, dark beer, tomato paste, chili powder, ground cumin, smoked paprika, dried oregano, salt, and black pepper.
5. Bring the chili to a simmer, then reduce the heat to low. Cover and let the chili simmer gently for about 30-40 minutes, stirring occasionally, to allow the flavors to meld together and the chili to thicken.
6. Taste the chili and adjust the seasoning with salt and black pepper if needed.

7. Once the elk chili is cooked to your desired consistency and flavor, remove it from the heat.
8. Serve the Devil's Tower elk chili hot, garnished with your favorite toppings such as shredded cheese, sour cream, chopped green onions, cilantro, or avocado slices.
9. Enjoy the hearty and flavorful elk chili inspired by the majestic Devil's Tower, perfect for warming up on a chilly day!

Cowboy Cobbler

Ingredients:

For the Filling:

- 4 cups sliced peaches (fresh or canned)
- 1 cup fresh or frozen blackberries
- 1/2 cup granulated sugar
- 2 tablespoons cornstarch
- 1 teaspoon ground cinnamon
- 1/2 teaspoon ground nutmeg
- 1 tablespoon lemon juice
- 1 teaspoon vanilla extract

For the Cobbler Topping:

- 1 cup all-purpose flour
- 1/2 cup granulated sugar
- 1 teaspoon baking powder
- 1/4 teaspoon salt
- 1/2 cup unsalted butter, melted
- 1/4 cup milk
- 1 teaspoon vanilla extract

Instructions:

1. Preheat your oven to 375°F (190°C). Grease a 9x13-inch baking dish with butter or non-stick cooking spray.
2. In a large bowl, combine the sliced peaches, blackberries, granulated sugar, cornstarch, ground cinnamon, ground nutmeg, lemon juice, and vanilla extract. Toss until the fruit is evenly coated. Transfer the fruit mixture to the prepared baking dish and spread it out into an even layer.
3. In another bowl, whisk together the all-purpose flour, granulated sugar, baking powder, and salt for the cobbler topping.
4. Pour the melted butter, milk, and vanilla extract over the dry ingredients for the cobbler topping. Stir until just combined, being careful not to overmix.

5. Drop spoonfuls of the cobbler topping over the fruit filling in the baking dish, covering it as evenly as possible.
6. Bake the cowboy cobbler in the preheated oven for 35-40 minutes, or until the fruit is bubbly and the cobbler topping is golden brown and cooked through.
7. Remove the cobbler from the oven and let it cool slightly before serving.
8. Serve the cowboy cobbler warm, topped with a scoop of vanilla ice cream or a dollop of whipped cream, if desired.
9. Enjoy the delicious flavors of this classic cowboy cobbler, with its juicy fruit filling and tender cobbler topping, perfect for any occasion!

Wyoming Venison Sausage

Ingredients:

- 1 lb ground venison
- 1/4 lb pork fatback, diced (optional, for moisture and flavor)
- 1 tablespoon olive oil
- 2 cloves garlic, minced
- 1 teaspoon dried sage
- 1 teaspoon dried thyme
- 1/2 teaspoon dried rosemary
- 1/2 teaspoon dried marjoram
- 1/2 teaspoon dried oregano
- 1/2 teaspoon smoked paprika
- 1/2 teaspoon ground black pepper
- 1/2 teaspoon salt
- Natural sausage casings (if making links)

Instructions:

1. In a large mixing bowl, combine the ground venison with the diced pork fatback (if using).
2. In a small skillet, heat the olive oil over medium heat. Add the minced garlic and cook for 1-2 minutes, or until fragrant. Remove from heat and let it cool slightly.
3. Add the cooked garlic and all the dried herbs and spices to the bowl with the ground venison. Mix well until the seasonings are evenly distributed throughout the meat mixture.
4. If making sausage links, soak the natural sausage casings in warm water according to the package instructions.
5. If making sausage patties, skip to step 6. If making sausage links, continue with the following steps:
    - Thread one end of a sausage casing onto the nozzle of a sausage stuffer or funnel.
    - Gently push the casing onto the nozzle, leaving a few inches of casing hanging off the end.
    - Carefully push the meat mixture through the sausage stuffer or funnel, filling the casing evenly and avoiding air pockets.

- Continue filling the casing until you reach the desired length, then twist or tie off the end to secure the sausage links.
- Repeat the process with the remaining meat mixture and casings.

6. Whether making patties or links, once the sausage mixture is prepared, cover it and refrigerate for at least 1 hour to allow the flavors to meld together.
7. When ready to cook, heat a skillet or grill over medium-high heat. If making patties, shape the sausage mixture into rounds and cook in the skillet or on the grill until browned and cooked through, about 3-4 minutes per side.
8. If making links, cook the sausages in the skillet or on the grill, turning occasionally, until browned and cooked through, about 10-12 minutes total.
9. Once cooked, remove the Wyoming venison sausage from the skillet or grill and let them rest for a few minutes before serving.
10. Serve the venison sausage hot as a delicious and flavorful main dish, or use them in your favorite recipes such as pasta dishes, breakfast scrambles, or sandwiches.
11. Enjoy the rich and savory taste of homemade Wyoming venison sausage, made with lean and flavorful venison meat!

Bear Lake Raspberry Jam

Ingredients:

- 4 cups fresh raspberries (or frozen, thawed)
- 2 cups granulated sugar
- 2 tablespoons fresh lemon juice
- 1 teaspoon lemon zest (optional)

Instructions:

1. Rinse the raspberries under cold water and pat them dry with paper towels. Remove any stems or leaves and discard any overripe or spoiled berries.
2. In a large, heavy-bottomed pot, combine the raspberries, granulated sugar, fresh lemon juice, and lemon zest (if using). Stir gently to combine.
3. Place the pot over medium-high heat and bring the raspberry mixture to a boil, stirring frequently to prevent sticking or burning.
4. Once the mixture comes to a rolling boil, reduce the heat to medium-low and let it simmer, stirring occasionally, for about 20-25 minutes, or until the raspberries break down and the mixture thickens to a jam-like consistency.
5. To test if the jam is ready, place a small spoonful of the hot mixture onto a chilled plate and let it cool for a few seconds. Run your finger through the jam – if it leaves a trail and doesn't immediately flow back together, it's done.
6. Once the jam reaches the desired consistency, remove the pot from the heat and let it cool slightly.
7. If you prefer a smoother jam, you can use an immersion blender or potato masher to break down any remaining raspberry chunks.
8. While the jam is still hot, carefully pour it into clean, sterilized jars, leaving about 1/4 inch of headspace at the top.
9. Wipe the rims of the jars with a clean, damp cloth to remove any spills or residue. Place the lids on the jars and screw on the bands until fingertip tight.
10. Process the jars in a boiling water bath for 10 minutes to seal them properly. If you're not canning the jam for long-term storage, you can skip this step and simply refrigerate the jars once they've cooled.
11. Allow the Bear Lake raspberry jam to cool completely before labeling and storing it in a cool, dark place. Properly sealed jars can be stored in the pantry for up to a year, while opened jars should be refrigerated and consumed within a few weeks.

12. Enjoy the delicious taste of homemade Bear Lake raspberry jam spread on toast, biscuits, scones, or used as a topping for yogurt, ice cream, or pancakes!

Buffalo Burger Sliders

Ingredients:

- 1 lb ground buffalo meat
- 1 teaspoon Worcestershire sauce
- 1/2 teaspoon garlic powder
- 1/2 teaspoon onion powder
- 1/2 teaspoon smoked paprika
- Salt and black pepper, to taste
- Slider buns
- Toppings (lettuce, tomato slices, onion slices, cheese, pickles, etc.)
- Condiments (ketchup, mustard, mayonnaise, etc.)

Instructions:

1. In a large mixing bowl, combine the ground buffalo meat with Worcestershire sauce, garlic powder, onion powder, smoked paprika, salt, and black pepper. Mix well until the seasonings are evenly distributed throughout the meat.
2. Divide the seasoned buffalo meat into equal-sized portions and shape them into small patties, slightly larger than the size of your slider buns.
3. Heat a grill or grill pan over medium-high heat. Lightly oil the grill grates or pan to prevent sticking.
4. Place the buffalo burger patties on the hot grill or grill pan and cook for about 3-4 minutes on each side, or until they reach your desired level of doneness.
5. During the last minute of cooking, you can add cheese slices on top of the patties to melt, if desired.
6. While the buffalo burger patties are cooking, lightly toast the slider buns on the grill or in a toaster oven until they are warm and golden brown.
7. Once the buffalo burger patties are cooked to perfection, remove them from the grill or grill pan and let them rest for a few minutes.
8. Assemble the buffalo burger sliders by placing a buffalo burger patty on the bottom half of each slider bun.
9. Add your favorite toppings and condiments to the sliders, such as lettuce, tomato slices, onion slices, pickles, ketchup, mustard, or mayonnaise.
10. Place the top half of the slider buns on top of the toppings to complete the sliders.

11. Serve the buffalo burger sliders hot, and enjoy these delicious and flavorful mini burgers as a tasty appetizer, snack, or meal!

Wyoming Whiskey Glazed Salmon

Ingredients:

- 4 salmon fillets (about 6 ounces each), skin-on
- Salt and black pepper, to taste
- 1 tablespoon olive oil

For the Wyoming Whiskey Glaze:

- 1/4 cup Wyoming whiskey (or any whiskey of your choice)
- 1/4 cup maple syrup
- 2 tablespoons soy sauce
- 1 tablespoon Dijon mustard
- 1 tablespoon Worcestershire sauce
- 2 cloves garlic, minced
- 1 teaspoon grated fresh ginger
- 1/2 teaspoon smoked paprika
- 1/4 teaspoon red pepper flakes (optional, for heat)
- Chopped fresh parsley, for garnish (optional)
- Lemon wedges, for serving

Instructions:

1. Preheat your grill to medium-high heat, or preheat your oven to 400°F (200°C).
2. Pat the salmon fillets dry with paper towels and season both sides with salt and black pepper.
3. In a small saucepan, combine all the ingredients for the Wyoming whiskey glaze: Wyoming whiskey, maple syrup, soy sauce, Dijon mustard, Worcestershire sauce, minced garlic, grated fresh ginger, smoked paprika, and red pepper flakes (if using). Stir to combine.
4. Place the saucepan over medium heat and bring the glaze to a simmer. Let it cook for 5-7 minutes, stirring occasionally, until it thickens slightly.
5. Remove the saucepan from the heat and set aside.
6. If grilling the salmon, lightly oil the grill grates. If baking, line a baking sheet with parchment paper or aluminum foil for easy cleanup.
7. Brush the salmon fillets lightly with olive oil to prevent sticking.
8. Place the salmon fillets on the grill or baking sheet, skin-side down.

9. Grill or bake the salmon for about 4-5 minutes per side, or until the fish is cooked through and flakes easily with a fork.
10. During the last few minutes of cooking, brush the Wyoming whiskey glaze over the salmon fillets, allowing it to caramelize and form a sticky glaze.
11. Once the salmon is cooked and glazed to perfection, remove it from the grill or oven.
12. Serve the Wyoming whiskey glazed salmon hot, garnished with chopped fresh parsley (if using) and lemon wedges on the side for squeezing.
13. Enjoy the sweet and savory flavors of this delicious glazed salmon, infused with the rich aroma of Wyoming whiskey!

Buffalo Steak Fajitas

Ingredients:

- 1 lb buffalo steak (such as sirloin or flank), thinly sliced against the grain
- 2 bell peppers (any color), sliced
- 1 large onion, sliced
- 2 cloves garlic, minced
- 2 tablespoons olive oil
- 2 tablespoons fajita seasoning (store-bought or homemade)
- Salt and black pepper, to taste
- Flour or corn tortillas, for serving
- Optional toppings: salsa, guacamole, sour cream, shredded cheese, chopped cilantro, lime wedges

Instructions:

1. In a large bowl, combine the sliced buffalo steak with minced garlic, fajita seasoning, salt, and black pepper. Toss well to coat the meat evenly with the seasonings.
2. Heat one tablespoon of olive oil in a large skillet or cast-iron pan over medium-high heat. Add the sliced bell peppers and onions to the skillet and cook, stirring occasionally, until they are softened and slightly charred, about 5-7 minutes. Remove the cooked vegetables from the skillet and set aside.
3. In the same skillet, add another tablespoon of olive oil. Add the seasoned buffalo steak slices to the skillet in a single layer, making sure not to overcrowd the pan. Cook the steak slices for 2-3 minutes on each side, or until they are browned and cooked to your desired level of doneness.
4. Once the buffalo steak slices are cooked, return the cooked vegetables to the skillet and toss everything together to combine.
5. Warm the tortillas in a separate skillet or in the microwave until they are soft and pliable.
6. Serve the buffalo steak fajitas hot, with warmed tortillas and your choice of toppings such as salsa, guacamole, sour cream, shredded cheese, chopped cilantro, and lime wedges.
7. Assemble the fajitas by spooning some of the buffalo steak and vegetable mixture onto each tortilla, then adding your favorite toppings.

8. Roll up the tortillas tightly to form fajitas and enjoy the delicious flavors of these buffalo steak fajitas, perfect for a quick and flavorful meal!

Jackson Hole Bison Tenderloin

Ingredients:

- 2 lbs bison tenderloin
- 2 tablespoons olive oil
- 2 cloves garlic, minced
- 1 tablespoon fresh thyme leaves
- 1 tablespoon fresh rosemary leaves
- Salt and black pepper, to taste

For the Red Wine Reduction Sauce:

- 1 cup red wine
- 1/2 cup beef or bison broth
- 2 tablespoons unsalted butter
- Salt and black pepper, to taste

Instructions:

1. Preheat your oven to 400°F (200°C).
2. In a small bowl, mix together the olive oil, minced garlic, fresh thyme leaves, and fresh rosemary leaves to create a marinade for the bison tenderloin.
3. Pat the bison tenderloin dry with paper towels and season it generously with salt and black pepper.
4. Rub the marinade all over the bison tenderloin, coating it evenly. Let the tenderloin marinate for at least 30 minutes at room temperature, or refrigerate it for up to 4 hours for maximum flavor.
5. Heat an oven-proof skillet or cast-iron pan over medium-high heat. Once hot, add the bison tenderloin to the skillet and sear it on all sides until browned, about 2-3 minutes per side.
6. Transfer the skillet to the preheated oven and roast the bison tenderloin for about 15-20 minutes, or until it reaches your desired level of doneness. The internal temperature should register 130-135°F (54-57°C) for medium-rare or 140-145°F (60-63°C) for medium.
7. Remove the skillet from the oven and transfer the bison tenderloin to a cutting board. Cover it loosely with aluminum foil and let it rest for 10 minutes before slicing.

8. While the bison tenderloin is resting, prepare the red wine reduction sauce. In the same skillet used to cook the tenderloin, place the skillet over medium heat. Add the red wine and beef or bison broth to the skillet, scraping up any browned bits from the bottom of the pan.
9. Let the sauce simmer and reduce by half, stirring occasionally, about 5-7 minutes.
10. Once the sauce has thickened slightly, remove the skillet from the heat and stir in the unsalted butter until melted. Season the sauce with salt and black pepper to taste.
11. Slice the rested bison tenderloin against the grain into thick slices.
12. Serve the Jackson Hole bison tenderloin slices hot, drizzled with the red wine reduction sauce, and accompanied by your favorite side dishes such as roasted vegetables, mashed potatoes, or a fresh green salad.
13. Enjoy the tender and flavorful Jackson Hole bison tenderloin, cooked to perfection and complemented by a rich red wine reduction sauce!

Sagebrush Grilled Quail

Ingredients:

- 4 whole quails, cleaned and giblets removed
- 1/4 cup olive oil
- 2 cloves garlic, minced
- 2 tablespoons fresh sage leaves, chopped
- 1 tablespoon fresh thyme leaves
- 1 tablespoon fresh rosemary leaves
- 1 teaspoon smoked paprika
- Salt and black pepper, to taste
- Lemon wedges, for serving

Instructions:

1. Preheat your grill to medium-high heat.
2. In a small bowl, combine the olive oil, minced garlic, chopped sage leaves, thyme leaves, rosemary leaves, smoked paprika, salt, and black pepper to create a marinade for the quail.
3. Pat the quails dry with paper towels and place them in a shallow dish or large resealable plastic bag.
4. Pour the marinade over the quails, turning them to coat evenly. Marinate the quails for at least 30 minutes at room temperature, or refrigerate them for up to 4 hours for maximum flavor.
5. Remove the quails from the marinade and let any excess drip off.
6. Place the quails on the preheated grill and cook for about 5-7 minutes per side, or until they are golden brown and cooked through. The internal temperature of the quails should reach 165°F (74°C) when measured with a meat thermometer.
7. While grilling, baste the quails with any remaining marinade to keep them moist and flavorful.
8. Once the quails are cooked through, remove them from the grill and let them rest for a few minutes before serving.
9. Serve the sagebrush grilled quail hot, garnished with fresh sage leaves and lemon wedges on the side for squeezing.
10. Enjoy the succulent and aromatic flavor of these sagebrush grilled quails, perfect for a special outdoor meal or gathering!

Buffalo Bolognese

Ingredients:

- 1 lb ground buffalo meat
- 2 tablespoons olive oil
- 1 onion, finely chopped
- 2 carrots, finely chopped
- 2 celery stalks, finely chopped
- 3 cloves garlic, minced
- 1 can (28 oz) crushed tomatoes
- 1/2 cup red wine (optional)
- 1 cup beef or vegetable broth
- 1 teaspoon dried oregano
- 1 teaspoon dried basil
- 1/2 teaspoon dried thyme
- Salt and black pepper, to taste
- 1/4 cup fresh parsley, chopped (for garnish)
- Grated Parmesan cheese, for serving
- Cooked pasta of your choice (spaghetti, fettuccine, penne, etc.)

Instructions:

1. Heat olive oil in a large skillet or Dutch oven over medium heat. Add the chopped onion, carrots, and celery, and cook until softened, about 5-7 minutes.
2. Add the minced garlic to the skillet and cook for an additional 1-2 minutes, until fragrant.
3. Push the vegetables to the side of the skillet and add the ground buffalo meat. Cook, breaking up the meat with a spoon, until browned and cooked through, about 5-7 minutes.
4. Once the buffalo meat is cooked, pour in the crushed tomatoes, red wine (if using), and beef or vegetable broth. Stir to combine.
5. Add the dried oregano, dried basil, dried thyme, salt, and black pepper to the skillet, and stir well to incorporate the seasonings into the sauce.
6. Bring the sauce to a simmer, then reduce the heat to low. Cover and let it simmer gently for about 30 minutes to allow the flavors to meld together and the sauce to thicken.
7. While the sauce is simmering, cook the pasta according to the package instructions until al dente. Drain and set aside.

8. Once the sauce has thickened to your desired consistency, taste and adjust the seasoning with salt and black pepper if needed.
9. Serve the buffalo bolognese over the cooked pasta, garnished with chopped fresh parsley and grated Parmesan cheese.
10. Enjoy the hearty and flavorful buffalo bolognese sauce, served over pasta for a delicious and satisfying meal!

Wyoming Whiskey Smoked Brisket

Ingredients:

- 1 whole brisket, about 10-12 pounds, trimmed of excess fat
- 1/4 cup kosher salt
- 1/4 cup coarsely ground black pepper
- 1/4 cup smoked paprika
- 1/4 cup brown sugar
- 1/4 cup Wyoming Whiskey (or your favorite whiskey)
- Wood chips or chunks for smoking (hickory, oak, or mesquite)

Instructions:

1. In a small bowl, combine the kosher salt, black pepper, smoked paprika, and brown sugar to make the dry rub.
2. Pat the brisket dry with paper towels. Rub the dry rub mixture all over the brisket, covering it evenly on all sides. Wrap the brisket tightly in plastic wrap and refrigerate for at least 4 hours, or overnight, to allow the flavors to penetrate the meat.
3. Remove the brisket from the refrigerator and let it sit at room temperature for about 1 hour before smoking.
4. Prepare your smoker according to manufacturer instructions and preheat it to 225-250°F (107-121°C). Add wood chips or chunks to the smoker box or directly to the coals for smoke flavor.
5. Place the brisket on the smoker rack, fat side up, and close the lid.
6. Smoke the brisket for about 1 hour per pound, or until the internal temperature reaches 195-205°F (90-96°C) and the meat is tender and easily pulls apart with a fork.
7. During the smoking process, you can periodically baste the brisket with Wyoming Whiskey to enhance the flavor and moisture.
8. Once the brisket is done, remove it from the smoker and let it rest for at least 30 minutes before slicing.
9. Slice the brisket against the grain into thin slices and serve hot.

This Wyoming Whiskey smoked brisket is rich, flavorful, and perfect for serving at gatherings, BBQs, or special occasions. Serve it with your favorite BBQ sauce, coleslaw, and cornbread for a complete and satisfying meal. Enjoy the delicious flavors of Wyoming whiskey-infused brisket!

Grand Teton Elk Stew

Ingredients:

- 2 pounds elk stew meat, cubed
- 2 tablespoons vegetable oil
- 1 onion, diced
- 2 cloves garlic, minced
- 2 carrots, peeled and sliced
- 2 celery stalks, sliced
- 2 potatoes, peeled and diced
- 4 cups beef broth
- 1 cup red wine (optional)
- 1 can (14.5 ounces) diced tomatoes
- 1 teaspoon dried thyme
- 1 teaspoon dried rosemary
- Salt and pepper to taste
- Fresh parsley, chopped, for garnish

Instructions:

1. In a large pot or Dutch oven, heat the vegetable oil over medium-high heat.
2. Add the cubed elk stew meat to the pot and brown on all sides, about 5-7 minutes. Remove the meat from the pot and set it aside.
3. In the same pot, add the diced onion and cook until softened, about 3-4 minutes. Add the minced garlic and cook for an additional 1-2 minutes.
4. Add the sliced carrots, celery, and diced potatoes to the pot, stirring to combine.
5. Return the browned elk meat to the pot.
6. Pour in the beef broth and red wine (if using), stirring to combine.
7. Add the diced tomatoes, including their juices, to the pot.
8. Stir in the dried thyme and dried rosemary, along with salt and pepper to taste.
9. Bring the stew to a simmer, then reduce the heat to low. Cover and let it simmer for 1-2 hours, stirring occasionally, until the elk meat is tender and the vegetables are cooked through.
10. Taste and adjust the seasoning as needed.
11. Serve the Grand Teton Elk Stew hot, garnished with chopped fresh parsley.

This Grand Teton Elk Stew is a comforting and satisfying meal that's perfect for cold winter days or cozy evenings by the fire. Serve it with crusty bread or biscuits for a complete and hearty meal. Enjoy the flavors of the Rocky Mountains with this delicious stew!

Green River Catfish Nuggets

Ingredients:

- 1 pound catfish nuggets
- 1 cup buttermilk
- 1 cup cornmeal
- 1/2 cup all-purpose flour
- 1 teaspoon salt
- 1/2 teaspoon black pepper
- 1/2 teaspoon paprika
- Vegetable oil for frying
- Lemon wedges for serving
- Tartar sauce or cocktail sauce for dipping (optional)

Instructions:

1. Place the catfish nuggets in a bowl and cover them with buttermilk. Let them soak in the buttermilk for at least 30 minutes, or up to 1 hour in the refrigerator. This helps tenderize the catfish and adds flavor.
2. In a shallow dish, combine the cornmeal, flour, salt, pepper, and paprika. Mix well to combine.
3. Heat vegetable oil in a deep fryer or large skillet to 350°F (175°C).
4. Remove the catfish nuggets from the buttermilk and dredge them in the cornmeal mixture, coating them evenly on all sides.
5. Carefully add the breaded catfish nuggets to the hot oil in batches, being careful not to overcrowd the fryer.
6. Fry the catfish nuggets for 3-4 minutes, or until they are golden brown and crispy, flipping them halfway through cooking for even browning.
7. Once the catfish nuggets are cooked through and crispy, remove them from the oil using a slotted spoon and transfer them to a plate lined with paper towels to drain any excess oil.
8. Serve the Green River catfish nuggets hot, with lemon wedges for squeezing over the top and tartar sauce or cocktail sauce for dipping, if desired.

These Green River catfish nuggets are crispy on the outside and tender on the inside,

with a delicious flavor that pairs perfectly with tangy tartar sauce or zesty cocktail sauce. Enjoy them as a tasty appetizer or main course, and savor the flavors of the river at home!

Bison Taco Salad

Ingredients:

- 1 pound ground bison meat
- 1 tablespoon olive oil
- 1 onion, diced
- 2 cloves garlic, minced
- 1 tablespoon taco seasoning (store-bought or homemade)
- Salt and pepper to taste
- 6 cups chopped romaine lettuce
- 1 cup cherry tomatoes, halved
- 1 cup canned black beans, drained and rinsed
- 1 cup canned corn kernels, drained
- 1 avocado, diced
- 1/2 cup shredded cheddar cheese
- 1/4 cup chopped fresh cilantro (optional)
- 1 lime, cut into wedges
- Tortilla chips for serving

For the dressing:

- 1/4 cup sour cream
- 2 tablespoons salsa
- 1 tablespoon lime juice
- Salt and pepper to taste

Instructions:

1. Heat olive oil in a skillet over medium-high heat. Add diced onion and minced garlic, and sauté until softened and fragrant, about 3-4 minutes.
2. Add ground bison meat to the skillet and cook, breaking it up with a spatula, until browned and cooked through, about 5-7 minutes.
3. Stir in taco seasoning, salt, and pepper, and cook for an additional 2-3 minutes to allow the flavors to meld. Remove from heat and set aside.
4. In a small bowl, whisk together sour cream, salsa, lime juice, salt, and pepper to make the dressing. Set aside.
5. In a large salad bowl, combine chopped romaine lettuce, cherry tomatoes, black beans, corn kernels, diced avocado, shredded cheddar cheese, and chopped fresh cilantro (if using).

6. Add the cooked bison meat to the salad bowl and toss everything together until well combined.
7. Drizzle the dressing over the salad and toss again to coat everything evenly.
8. Serve the bison taco salad immediately, garnished with lime wedges and tortilla chips on the side for scooping.

This bison taco salad is a satisfying and delicious meal that's perfect for lunch or dinner. It's packed with protein, fiber, and flavor, and can be easily customized with your favorite toppings and dressings. Enjoy this nutritious twist on a classic favorite!

Wyoming Whiskey Peach Cobbler

Ingredients:

- 6 cups sliced ripe peaches (fresh or frozen)
- 1/4 cup Wyoming Whiskey (or bourbon)
- 1/2 cup granulated sugar
- 1 teaspoon vanilla extract
- 1 teaspoon ground cinnamon
- 1/4 teaspoon ground nutmeg
- 2 tablespoons cornstarch
- 1 tablespoon lemon juice

For the topping:

- 1 cup all-purpose flour
- 1/2 cup granulated sugar
- 1 teaspoon baking powder
- 1/4 teaspoon salt
- 1/2 cup cold unsalted butter, cut into small pieces
- 1/4 cup boiling water

Instructions:

1. Preheat your oven to 375°F (190°C). Grease a 9x13-inch baking dish or a similar-sized ovenproof dish.
2. In a large bowl, combine the sliced peaches, Wyoming Whiskey, granulated sugar, vanilla extract, ground cinnamon, ground nutmeg, cornstarch, and lemon juice. Stir gently until the peaches are evenly coated. Transfer the peach mixture to the prepared baking dish and spread it out into an even layer.
3. In a separate bowl, whisk together the all-purpose flour, granulated sugar, baking powder, and salt. Cut in the cold butter using a pastry cutter or fork until the mixture resembles coarse crumbs.
4. Pour the boiling water over the flour mixture and stir until just combined. The batter will be thick and sticky.
5. Drop spoonfuls of the batter evenly over the peaches in the baking dish, covering as much of the surface as possible.
6. Bake the cobbler in the preheated oven for 40-45 minutes, or until the topping is golden brown and the peach filling is bubbly.

7. Remove the cobbler from the oven and let it cool for a few minutes before serving.
8. Serve the Wyoming Whiskey peach cobbler warm, optionally topped with vanilla ice cream or whipped cream.

This Wyoming Whiskey peach cobbler is a wonderful way to enjoy the flavors of summer and whiskey. It's perfect for serving at gatherings, potlucks, or as a special treat for family and friends. Enjoy the delicious combination of sweet peaches and whiskey-infused goodness!

Bison Breakfast Hash

Ingredients:

- 1 pound ground bison
- 2 tablespoons olive oil
- 1 onion, diced
- 2 cloves garlic, minced
- 2 bell peppers, diced (any color)
- 2 medium potatoes, diced
- 1 teaspoon paprika
- 1 teaspoon dried thyme
- Salt and pepper to taste
- 4 eggs
- Chopped fresh parsley or green onions for garnish (optional)

Instructions:

1. Heat olive oil in a large skillet over medium-high heat.
2. Add diced potatoes to the skillet and cook, stirring occasionally, until they are golden brown and tender, about 10-12 minutes. Remove the potatoes from the skillet and set them aside.
3. In the same skillet, add ground bison and cook until browned and cooked through, breaking it up with a spatula as it cooks, about 5-7 minutes. Remove the bison from the skillet and set it aside.
4. Add diced onion, minced garlic, and diced bell peppers to the skillet. Cook until the vegetables are softened, about 3-4 minutes.
5. Return the cooked bison and potatoes to the skillet. Sprinkle paprika, dried thyme, salt, and pepper over the mixture. Stir to combine.
6. Create 4 wells in the hash mixture and crack an egg into each well.
7. Cover the skillet with a lid and cook until the eggs are cooked to your liking, about 5-7 minutes for runny yolks or longer for firmer yolks.
8. Once the eggs are cooked, remove the skillet from the heat. Sprinkle chopped fresh parsley or green onions over the top for garnish, if desired.
9. Serve the bison breakfast hash hot, dividing it into individual portions and serving each with a cooked egg on top.

This bison breakfast hash is a satisfying and delicious meal that's perfect for serving on weekend mornings or special occasions. It's packed with protein, vegetables, and flavor, making it a nutritious and filling breakfast option. Enjoy!

Devil's Tower Trout Cakes

Ingredients:

- 1 pound trout fillets, cooked and flaked (you can also use canned trout)
- 1/2 cup breadcrumbs
- 1/4 cup mayonnaise
- 2 tablespoons Dijon mustard
- 2 green onions, finely chopped
- 1/4 cup chopped fresh parsley
- 1 tablespoon lemon juice
- 1 teaspoon Old Bay seasoning (or your favorite seafood seasoning)
- Salt and pepper to taste
- 2 tablespoons olive oil, for frying
- Lemon wedges and tartar sauce for serving (optional)

Instructions:

1. In a large bowl, combine the cooked and flaked trout fillets, breadcrumbs, mayonnaise, Dijon mustard, chopped green onions, chopped fresh parsley, lemon juice, Old Bay seasoning, salt, and pepper. Mix well until all the ingredients are evenly combined.
2. Divide the trout mixture into equal portions and shape them into patties, about 1/2 to 3/4 inch thick.
3. Heat olive oil in a large skillet over medium heat.
4. Carefully place the trout cakes in the skillet and cook until golden brown and crispy on both sides, about 3-4 minutes per side.
5. Once cooked, transfer the trout cakes to a plate lined with paper towels to drain any excess oil.
6. Serve the Devil's Tower Trout Cakes hot, garnished with lemon wedges and tartar sauce on the side, if desired.

These Devil's Tower Trout Cakes are crispy on the outside and tender on the inside, with a delicious flavor that showcases the natural goodness of trout. They're perfect for serving as an appetizer, snack, or main course, and they pair well with a variety of side dishes. Enjoy this tasty dish inspired by the iconic Devil's Tower!

Wyoming Elk Meatballs

Ingredients:

- 1 pound ground elk meat
- 1/2 cup breadcrumbs
- 1/4 cup grated Parmesan cheese
- 1/4 cup finely chopped onion
- 2 cloves garlic, minced
- 1 egg
- 1 tablespoon Worcestershire sauce
- 1 teaspoon dried oregano
- 1 teaspoon dried thyme
- 1/2 teaspoon salt
- 1/4 teaspoon black pepper
- Olive oil, for cooking
- Marinara sauce, for serving (optional)
- Fresh parsley, chopped, for garnish (optional)

Instructions:

1. Preheat your oven to 375°F (190°C). Line a baking sheet with parchment paper or aluminum foil.
2. In a large mixing bowl, combine the ground elk meat, breadcrumbs, grated Parmesan cheese, chopped onion, minced garlic, egg, Worcestershire sauce, dried oregano, dried thyme, salt, and black pepper. Mix well until all the ingredients are evenly incorporated.
3. Shape the mixture into meatballs, using about 1 tablespoon of mixture for each meatball. Roll them between your palms to form round balls and place them on the prepared baking sheet.
4. Once all the meatballs are formed, lightly brush them with olive oil.
5. Bake the elk meatballs in the preheated oven for 20-25 minutes, or until they are cooked through and browned on the outside.
6. Once cooked, remove the meatballs from the oven and let them cool for a few minutes.
7. Serve the Wyoming elk meatballs hot, optionally with marinara sauce for dipping or pouring over the top, and garnish with chopped fresh parsley if desired.

These Wyoming elk meatballs are tender, juicy, and packed with flavor. They make a delicious appetizer, main course, or addition to pasta dishes or sandwiches. Enjoy the unique taste of elk meat with this tasty recipe!

Cowboy Cactus Salad

Ingredients:

- 2 prickly pear cactus pads (nopales), cleaned and diced
- 1 tomato, diced
- 1/2 red onion, finely chopped
- 1/4 cup chopped fresh cilantro
- 1 jalapeño pepper, seeded and finely chopped (optional)
- Juice of 1 lime
- Salt and pepper to taste
- Tortilla chips or corn tortillas for serving (optional)

Instructions:

1. Prepare the prickly pear cactus pads (nopales) by trimming off the edges and spines, then rinsing them under cold water to remove any remaining spines and sticky residue. Dice the cleaned cactus pads into small pieces.
2. In a medium bowl, combine the diced cactus pads, diced tomato, finely chopped red onion, chopped fresh cilantro, and seeded and chopped jalapeño pepper (if using).
3. Squeeze the juice of one lime over the salad mixture, and season with salt and pepper to taste.
4. Toss the salad gently to combine all the ingredients evenly.
5. Let the cowboy cactus salad sit for about 10-15 minutes to allow the flavors to meld together.
6. Serve the salad chilled, either on its own or with tortilla chips or corn tortillas for scooping.

This cowboy cactus salad is light, fresh, and bursting with flavors from the Southwest. It's perfect as a side dish for grilled meats or tacos, or as a refreshing appetizer on its own. Enjoy the unique taste and texture of prickly pear cactus in this delicious salad!

Sagebrush Smoked Trout Dip

Ingredients:

- 8 ounces smoked trout, skin removed and flaked
- 1/2 cup sour cream
- 1/4 cup mayonnaise
- 2 tablespoons freshly squeezed lemon juice
- 1 tablespoon chopped fresh chives
- 1 tablespoon chopped fresh dill
- 1 teaspoon Worcestershire sauce
- Salt and pepper to taste
- Sagebrush sprigs for smoking (optional)
- Crackers, bread, or vegetable sticks for serving

Instructions:

1. In a mixing bowl, combine the flaked smoked trout, sour cream, mayonnaise, lemon juice, chopped chives, chopped dill, and Worcestershire sauce. Mix well to combine.
2. Taste the dip and season with salt and pepper to your liking. Adjust the lemon juice or other seasonings as needed.
3. If you want to infuse the dip with sagebrush smoke flavor, you can do so by using a smoking gun or smoker. Place the sagebrush sprigs in the smoking chamber and light them. Once the chamber is filled with smoke, cover the bowl of dip with plastic wrap or a lid and allow it to sit for 5-10 minutes to absorb the smoke flavor.
4. After smoking (if desired), transfer the dip to a serving bowl and garnish with additional chopped chives or dill, if desired.
5. Serve the sagebrush smoked trout dip with crackers, bread, or vegetable sticks for dipping.

This sagebrush smoked trout dip is creamy, flavorful, and perfect for entertaining guests or enjoying as a special treat. The addition of sagebrush smoke adds a unique and aromatic element to the dip, elevating it to a whole new level. Enjoy the delicious flavors of the outdoors with this tasty appetizer!

Pinedale Pheasant Casserole

Ingredients:

- 2 pheasant breasts, cooked and shredded (you can also use pheasant thighs or a combination)
- 4 cups cooked egg noodles
- 1 can (10.5 ounces) condensed cream of mushroom soup
- 1/2 cup sour cream
- 1/2 cup milk
- 1 cup shredded cheddar cheese
- 1/2 cup diced onion
- 1/2 cup diced celery
- 1/2 cup diced bell pepper (any color)
- 1/4 cup chopped fresh parsley
- 2 cloves garlic, minced
- 1 teaspoon dried thyme
- 1/2 teaspoon dried sage
- Salt and pepper to taste
- 1 cup breadcrumbs
- 2 tablespoons butter, melted

Instructions:

1. Preheat your oven to 350°F (175°C). Grease a 9x13-inch baking dish or similar-sized casserole dish.
2. In a large mixing bowl, combine the cooked and shredded pheasant meat, cooked egg noodles, condensed cream of mushroom soup, sour cream, milk, shredded cheddar cheese, diced onion, diced celery, diced bell pepper, chopped fresh parsley, minced garlic, dried thyme, dried sage, salt, and pepper. Mix well until all ingredients are evenly combined.
3. Transfer the mixture to the prepared baking dish, spreading it out into an even layer.
4. In a small bowl, combine the breadcrumbs and melted butter, stirring until the breadcrumbs are evenly coated with butter.
5. Sprinkle the buttered breadcrumbs over the top of the casserole mixture in the baking dish.
6. Cover the baking dish with aluminum foil and bake in the preheated oven for 30 minutes.

7. After 30 minutes, remove the foil and continue baking for an additional 10-15 minutes, or until the breadcrumbs are golden brown and the casserole is heated through.
8. Once done, remove the casserole from the oven and let it cool for a few minutes before serving.
9. Serve the Pinedale pheasant casserole hot, garnished with additional chopped parsley if desired.

This Pinedale pheasant casserole is hearty, creamy, and packed with flavor, making it a perfect comfort food for chilly evenings or special occasions. Enjoy the delicious taste of Wyoming with this delightful dish!

Bear Lake Blueberry Pie

Ingredients:

For the crust:

- 2 1/2 cups all-purpose flour
- 1 tablespoon granulated sugar
- 1 teaspoon salt
- 1 cup unsalted butter, cold and cut into small cubes
- 6-8 tablespoons ice water

For the filling:

- 6 cups fresh blueberries, washed and dried
- 1/2 cup granulated sugar
- 1/4 cup cornstarch
- 1 tablespoon lemon juice
- 1 teaspoon vanilla extract
- Zest of 1 lemon
- 1 tablespoon unsalted butter, cut into small pieces
- Egg wash (1 egg beaten with 1 tablespoon water), for brushing

Instructions:

For the crust:

1. In a large mixing bowl, combine the flour, sugar, and salt.
2. Add the cold cubed butter to the flour mixture. Using a pastry cutter or your fingertips, work the butter into the flour until the mixture resembles coarse crumbs.
3. Gradually add the ice water, 1 tablespoon at a time, mixing with a fork until the dough just comes together.
4. Divide the dough into two equal portions, shape each portion into a disk, and wrap them tightly in plastic wrap. Refrigerate for at least 1 hour, or until firm.

For the filling:

1. In a large mixing bowl, combine the fresh blueberries, granulated sugar, cornstarch, lemon juice, vanilla extract, and lemon zest. Gently toss until the blueberries are evenly coated.

Assembly:

1. Preheat your oven to 375°F (190°C).
2. On a lightly floured surface, roll out one disk of dough into a circle large enough to line a 9-inch pie dish. Carefully transfer the dough to the pie dish, gently pressing it into the bottom and up the sides.
3. Pour the blueberry filling into the prepared pie crust, spreading it out into an even layer. Dot the top of the filling with pieces of unsalted butter.
4. Roll out the second disk of dough and place it over the filling. Trim any excess dough and crimp the edges to seal. Cut a few slits in the top crust to allow steam to escape.
5. Brush the top crust with the egg wash for a golden finish.
6. Place the pie on a baking sheet to catch any drips and bake in the preheated oven for 45-55 minutes, or until the crust is golden brown and the filling is bubbling.
7. If the edges of the crust start to brown too quickly, you can cover them with aluminum foil halfway through baking.
8. Once done, remove the pie from the oven and let it cool on a wire rack before slicing and serving.

This Bear Lake Blueberry Pie is best enjoyed warm with a scoop of vanilla ice cream or a dollop of whipped cream. It's a delightful dessert that captures the essence of summer with its sweet and tangy blueberry filling and flaky, buttery crust. Enjoy!

Buffalo Sloppy Joes

Ingredients:

- 1 pound ground buffalo meat (bison)
- 1 tablespoon olive oil
- 1/2 onion, finely diced
- 2 cloves garlic, minced
- 1/2 cup diced bell peppers (any color)
- 1/2 cup diced celery
- 1/2 cup buffalo sauce (such as Frank's RedHot)
- 1/4 cup ketchup
- 1 tablespoon Worcestershire sauce
- 1 tablespoon brown sugar
- 1 teaspoon smoked paprika
- Salt and pepper to taste
- Hamburger buns or sandwich rolls, for serving

Instructions:

1. Heat olive oil in a large skillet over medium heat. Add the ground buffalo meat and cook, breaking it up with a spatula, until browned and cooked through, about 5-7 minutes. Drain any excess fat if necessary.
2. Add the diced onion, minced garlic, diced bell peppers, and diced celery to the skillet with the cooked buffalo meat. Cook, stirring occasionally, until the vegetables are softened, about 5 minutes.
3. In a small bowl, whisk together the buffalo sauce, ketchup, Worcestershire sauce, brown sugar, smoked paprika, salt, and pepper.
4. Pour the buffalo sauce mixture over the cooked buffalo meat and vegetables in the skillet. Stir to combine, making sure the meat and vegetables are evenly coated in the sauce.
5. Reduce the heat to low and let the mixture simmer for 5-10 minutes, allowing the flavors to meld together and the sauce to thicken slightly.
6. Once done, remove the skillet from the heat.
7. Serve the buffalo sloppy joe mixture on hamburger buns or sandwich rolls, spooning it onto the bottom halves of the buns. Optionally, you can top with coleslaw, sliced pickles, or crumbled blue cheese for extra flavor.
8. Cover with the top halves of the buns and serve immediately.

These buffalo sloppy joes are flavorful, slightly spicy, and perfect for serving as a quick and easy weeknight meal or for a casual gathering with friends and family. Enjoy the bold and tangy taste of buffalo sauce in this delicious twist on a classic favorite!

Wyoming Whiskey Glazed Chicken

Ingredients:

- 4 boneless, skinless chicken breasts
- Salt and pepper to taste
- 1 tablespoon olive oil

For the Wyoming Whiskey glaze:

- 1/4 cup Wyoming Whiskey (or bourbon)
- 1/4 cup brown sugar
- 2 tablespoons soy sauce
- 2 tablespoons Worcestershire sauce
- 2 cloves garlic, minced
- 1 teaspoon Dijon mustard
- 1/2 teaspoon smoked paprika
- 1/4 teaspoon ground black pepper
- Chopped fresh parsley for garnish (optional)

Instructions:

1. Season the chicken breasts with salt and pepper to taste.
2. In a large skillet, heat olive oil over medium-high heat. Add the chicken breasts to the skillet and cook until browned on both sides and cooked through, about 6-8 minutes per side, depending on thickness. Remove the chicken from the skillet and set it aside.
3. In the same skillet, reduce the heat to medium. Add the Wyoming Whiskey, brown sugar, soy sauce, Worcestershire sauce, minced garlic, Dijon mustard, smoked paprika, and ground black pepper. Stir to combine.
4. Allow the sauce to simmer and thicken for 3-5 minutes, stirring occasionally.
5. Return the cooked chicken breasts to the skillet, turning them to coat them evenly in the whiskey glaze. Cook for an additional 2-3 minutes, allowing the chicken to absorb the flavors of the glaze.
6. Once done, remove the skillet from the heat.
7. Serve the Wyoming Whiskey glazed chicken hot, garnished with chopped fresh parsley if desired.

This Wyoming Whiskey glazed chicken is tender, juicy, and bursting with flavor. The sweet and savory glaze adds depth to the dish, making it perfect for serving as a main course with your favorite side dishes. Enjoy the delicious taste of Wyoming Whiskey in this mouthwatering chicken dish!

Bighorn Basin Bison Kabobs

Ingredients:

- 1 pound bison sirloin or ribeye steak, cut into 1-inch cubes
- 1 red bell pepper, cut into chunks
- 1 green bell pepper, cut into chunks
- 1 yellow bell pepper, cut into chunks
- 1 red onion, cut into chunks
- 8-10 cherry tomatoes
- 8-10 cremini mushrooms, cleaned and stems removed
- Wooden or metal skewers

For the marinade:

- 1/4 cup olive oil
- 2 tablespoons balsamic vinegar
- 2 cloves garlic, minced
- 1 teaspoon dried thyme
- 1 teaspoon dried rosemary
- 1/2 teaspoon smoked paprika
- Salt and pepper to taste

Instructions:

1. In a small bowl, whisk together the olive oil, balsamic vinegar, minced garlic, dried thyme, dried rosemary, smoked paprika, salt, and pepper to make the marinade.
2. Place the bison cubes in a large resealable plastic bag or shallow dish. Pour the marinade over the bison, making sure it's evenly coated. Seal the bag or cover the dish, and marinate the bison in the refrigerator for at least 30 minutes, or up to 4 hours, turning occasionally.
3. While the bison is marinating, soak wooden skewers in water for at least 30 minutes to prevent them from burning on the grill.
4. Preheat your grill to medium-high heat.
5. Thread the marinated bison cubes onto the skewers, alternating with chunks of bell peppers, red onion, cherry tomatoes, and cremini mushrooms.
6. Once the grill is hot, place the kabobs on the grill grates and cook for 8-10 minutes, turning occasionally, or until the bison is cooked to your desired doneness and the vegetables are tender and slightly charred.

7. Remove the kabobs from the grill and let them rest for a few minutes before serving.
8. Serve the Bighorn Basin bison kabobs hot, garnished with chopped fresh parsley or cilantro if desired.

These Bighorn Basin bison kabobs are juicy, tender, and packed with flavor from the marinade and grilled vegetables. They're perfect for summer cookouts, gatherings, or anytime you want to enjoy a delicious and satisfying meal. Enjoy the taste of Wyoming with these mouthwatering kabobs!

www.ingramcontent.com/pod-product-compliance
Lightning Source LLC
LaVergne TN
LVHW081609060526
838201LV00054B/2168